A Passover Haggadah for Christians

"And you shall tell your son on that day, 'It is because of what the LORD did for me when I came out of Egypt.'" [Exodus 13:8]

A Passover Haggadah for Christians

Bruce Fingerhut

ST. AUGUSTINE'S PRESS
South Bend, Indiana

Manufactured in the United States of America

1 2 3 4 5 6   16 15 14 13 12 11

Library of Congress Cataloging in Publication Data
Fingerhut, Bruce, 1943–
A Passover Haggadah for Christians / Bruce Fingerhut.
p. cm.
ISBN 978-1-58731-638-8 (paperbound: alk. paper)
1. Passover – Christian observance. 2. Lord's Supper.
3. Haggadah – Adaptations. 4. Seder – Liturgy – Texts. I. Title.
BV199.P25F56 2011
265'.9 – dc22   2011009425

∞ The paper used in this publication meets the minimum
requirements of the American National Standard for Information
Sciences – Permanence of Paper for Printed Materials, ANSI
Z39.48-1984.

ST. AUGUSTINE'S PRESS
www.staugustine.net

Preface

I remember reading a lot of Lenin in graduate school, and after several works the strongest reaction I had was that he was not really narrating the way the world *was*, nor was he simply outlining a plan for the future. Rather, he was speaking about the future that he thought himself *already to occupy*, as though he were somehow ahead of us, *pulling* us into the future, a future that was, for him, the only true reality, whereas contemporary time, the one occupied by everyone else, was merely a transitory (and, therefore, in the end, an unreal) way-station.

Now what does all this have to do with a Passover Haggadah for Christians? It is this: just as it seemed to me that Lenin's manner was exactly the wrong way to understand the past (i.e., as a prequel to the present/future), so too it is wrong of us as Christians not to take the Haggadah, the outline for the service of the Passover, *on its own terms*, rather than solely as an explanation for certain words or actions of Jesus.

There is a special delight in understanding, say, the story of the Tower of Babel on its own terms, even though it may be understood more deeply by knowing the story of Pentecost. But nevertheless, understanding something in the right order is wonderfully mind-opening.

It is easy, but, I contend, profoundly wrong, to read the Old Testament as but a preparation to the New Testament. St. Augustine wrote of the two Testaments that the New lies hidden in the Old, and the Old is made manifest in the New. Jesus himself was constantly quoting the Old Testament as the authoritative text for understanding his own calling and his own teachings. We must ask, then, why *we* should view the Old Testament as anything less?

This Haggadah is an authentic one, not one made up merely to explain the Last Supper. It could be used by Jewish families for Passover, though they would likely not use the additional materials meant to bring it to the Christian context. None of the words are "reinterpreted" to conform to a pre-decided Christian viewpoint. You will see soon enough that that is not necessary, and when it is *not necessary* to do this, I believe it is *necessary not* to do it. What was handed down to the Jews is handed down to the Christians, and there is no need to alter the text in any way for the message of redemption to shine through clearly.

Both Passover and Easter concern the central event in history: the God-incursion into the life of man, and the freely given pathway to a moral, happy, and fulfilled life in God. And though, of necessity, the terms of the redemptive acts of God and the nature of freedom differ in Passover from Easter, the likenesses between the two are sufficient to edify us, encourage us, and, most of all, remind us of the essential similarities.

The closeness between Passover and Easter, not only of these themes and purposes but also of the events themselves, should rekindle in Christians and Jews a mutual understanding and even care. Often, it has not.

Passover, like Easter, after all, is about redemption and covenant. Passover ends with a covenant between man and God at Sinai; Easter with a new redemption and a new covenant with God. Biblical events that antedated Passover and Easter also have similarities, on the one hand with God's appearing to Moses, revealing his name, and commissioning him to be his agent in freeing his people; and on the other with Jesus' triumphal return to Jerusalem on Palm Sunday, leading up to the Last Supper, a Passover Seder. The events of Passover recounted in the Haggadah are easily seen as similar to events of the New Testament, particularly of Easter but also of other events in Jesus' life: slaying of the first-born, the darkness falling over the land, the nature of blood sacrifice, the defiance of an alien king, the signaling out of a time as unique in history . . . indeed, the very way in which historical time is "started" or counted; the final call for "Next Year in Jerusalem" – Jerusalem, the place of Jesus' triumph and death – and these examples are but a few. Again, the consonance of these events should lead both Jews and Christians to a greater understanding, even sympathy, for one another. I pray that this Haggadah will be a small gesture in that understanding.

A Mercifully Short Biography

Bruce Fingerhut was born in Washington, D.C., and was raised in the Washington Metropolitan area in a Jewish household. He converted and was baptized just prior to his twenty-ninth year, after coming to the conclusion that the world did not make sense without Jesus Christ. With that great help, he has been seeking to make sense of it ever since. He founded and heads St. Augustine's Press.

A Passover Haggadah for Christians

Observe the month of Abib, and keep the passover to the LORD your God; for in the month of Abib the LORD your God brought you out of Egypt by night. And you shall offer the passover sacrifice to the LORD your God, from the flock or the herd, at the place which the LORD will choose, to make his name dwell there. You shall eat no leavened bread with it; seven days you shall eat it with un-leavened bread, the bread of affliction – for you came out of the land of Egypt in hurried flight – that all the days of your life you may remember the day when you came out of the land of Egypt. [Deuteronomy 16:1–3]

Introductory Note

The Haggadah is the prayer book containing the text for the order of service for the Passover ritual meal, or seder. It was completed sometime in the 2nd century A.D., and there are several variations of it. But the general overall purpose in all the versions is the same, to recount the greatest event in Jewish history, the exodus from Egypt, which occurred in the 13th century B.C. (though there are several competing theories of when exactly these events occurred in history) and culmi-nated in God's bestowing on Moses the Ten Commandments at Mt. Horeb (also known as Mt. Sinai). As recounted in the book of Exodus, this was followed by the Hebrew people's forty years of wandering in the desert until a new generation of leadership took over (this for the transgression of worship-ing a golden calf [see Exodus 32]). They then crossed into Canaan, the "land flowing with milk and honey."

The Haggadah tells the story of the actual exodus, or "going-forth," and reminds the participants of the plagues visited upon the Egyptians to force Pharaoh (Ramses II) to release the Hebrews from their captivity in Egypt. It also recounts several theories about the meaning of these events in history.

This Haggadah retains all the central prayers and explanations, but in an easy-to-follow style; it also offers a wider explanation in light of the epiphany of Christ. None of the materials in a typical Haggadah are in any way distorted, nor is any significant portion of the Haggadah left out. The many parts of the Haggadah that refer to scriptural passages now have the citations.

It should be noted that to recite the *entire* haggadah and perform all the actions in it will take several hours to complete. Many seders are of shorter length, so material of lesser import for our understanding of the service has been put in smaller type and may be omitted.

All quotations from the Bible are in the Revised Standard Version translation; these quotations employ the spellings, capitalization, and punctuation of the RSV.

Key to Using the Haggadah

The Haggadah is a prayer book (really, from the point of view of observant Jews, a "telling," or narrative, that communally recalls the exodus), and thus is meant to be read aloud. However, not *all* the words of this Haggadah are to be read aloud, since it contains directions and commentary. The seder service itself begins on page 1.

A Seder is meant to be communal and didactic, and the leader often directs the participation from many or all at the table. Here is a key to the markings and aids in this Haggadah.

✡ x ✝

[bracketed words]	For scriptural quotes and references.
Italic	These serve several purposes: as subheads, for foreign words, and for directions.
blue italics	For commentary. It is up to the participants whether or not these should be read aloud. Most of the commentary gives the Christian context to the seder.
underlined words	Used in just a few prayers to designate words that should be read aloud at certain specified times.
Hebrew	Hebrew (always with a translation into English and always with an English transliteration) is employed for a selected number of important prayers, which for the most part are either communal prayers or said by someone other than the leader. A decision as to whether these words are to be read aloud or in silence should be made prior to beginning the service.
SMALL CAPS	Used to give directions for major actions, e.g., washing the hands drinking a cup of wine, etc.
footnotes	For minor commentary and longer scriptural quotations.
smaller type	For passages of lesser importance, which may be skipped for a shortened seder service.

Pre-Seder Preparations

A Word about Leaven
One act of preparation, often, as here, one that has already occurred prior to the seder service itself, though many people perform these actions as an integral part of the seder, involves the search and removal of all leaven from the house, to prepare for the feast of unleavened bread. In footnote 12 on pages 24–25, leaven's role is seen in moral, as well as the historical, terms. For the moment, let us quote the Old Testament admonition ("Seven days you shall eat unleavened bread; on the first day you shall put away leaven out of your houses, for if any one eats what is leavened, from the first day until the seventh day, that person shall be cut off from Israel." [Exodus 12:15]) and the New Testament explanation ("Your boasting is not good. Do you not know that a little leaven leavens the whole lump? Cleanse out the old leaven that you may be a new lump, as you really are unleavened. For Christ, our paschal lamb, has been sacrificed. Let us, therefore, celebrate the festival, not with the old leaven, the leaven of malice and evil, but with the unleavened bread of sincerity and truth." [1 Corinthians 5:6–8]).

The Table and Seating
Part of the ritual itself is that all the people are "reclined" at table. In modern times this usually means that a pillow or cushion is placed at the back and side of the chair, at least for the leader but often for each person at the table. On the table itself or, if needed, a sideboard, is placed a bowl of water and a towel to wash the hands, several bowls of salted water to dip the karpas (see below), a plate with three sheets of matzah, each separated by a napkin or cloth, with the entire contents then covered. The middle matzah will be broken in half, with one half, the afikomen [ah' fee co' men], separated and served as the last item to be eaten at the seder. The top matzah and half of the second are eaten early in the seder for the blessing

over bread. The bottom one is eaten later as the "Hillel sandwich" (see below). A bottle or more of wine is placed on the table, and each participant has a wine glass filled with wine. At the center of the table is a wine glass filled with wine, the Cup of Elijah (in some traditions, the cup is filled at a later time, when the third cup is filled for the participants). Fully visible to all participants is the Seder Plate.

The Seder Plate
In the center of the table there will be a Seder Plate, containing five items, which are listed below in their order of use at the seder, from the point of view of the leader:

1. Bitter herbs (*maror* and *chazeret*); *maror* is typically horseradish, though other bitter herbs suffice, representing the bitter life suffered by the Hebrew people under the Egyptians; *chazeret* is typically romaine lettuce, whose roots are bitter, and may be substituted for *maror*.

2. *Charoses*, a mixture of wine, nuts, fruit (usually apples), and sometimes raisins, with cinnamon and sugar, representing the straw-less mortar Pharaoh demanded the Hebrews use to make bricks [see Exodus 5].

3. Vegetables other than bitter herbs (*karpas*), usually parsley, but also celery, lettuce, onion, or potatoes can be used. Whichever one is used, it is dipped in salt water (representing tears) as a symbol of the simple but painful life suffered by the Hebrews under Egyptian affliction.

4. Roasted lamb shank bone (*z'roa*), representing the sacrifice of the lamb and the smearing of lamb's blood on the gate posts or lintels of the homes [see Exodus 12].

5. Hard-boiled or roasted egg (*beitzah*), representing the festival sacrifice that was offered at the Temple in Jerusalem and eaten as a part of the seder meal there. It is a symbol

of mourning (eggs being the first thing served to mourners after funerals), in this case symbolizing the mourning of the destruction of the Temple.

The Order of the Passover Seder

Here is the complete order of the seder:

I. *Kadeish (the blessings and first cup of wine)*
II. *Ur'chatz (washing the hands)*
III. *Karpas (appetizer)*
IV. *Yachatz (breaking the middle matzah)*
V. *Magid (the telling)*
    1. *Ha Lachma Anya (invitation to seder)*
    2. *Mah Nistanah (The Four Questions)*
    3. *The Four Sons*
    4. *"Go and learn"*
    5. *Kos Sheini (second cup of wine)*
VI. *Rohtzah (ritual washing of hands)*
VII. *Motzi ("who brings forth")*
VIII. *Matzo (blessing of the matzah)*
IX. *Maror (bitter herbs)*
X. *Koreich (the Hillel sandwich)*
XI. *Shulchan Orech (the meal)*
XII. *Tzafun (eating the afikomen)*
XIII. *Boreich (grace after meals)*
    1. *Kos Shlishi (the third cup of wine*
    2. *Kos shel Eliyahu ha-Navi (Cup of Elijah)*
XIV. *Hallel (songs of praise)*
XV. *Nirtzah (concluding song and prayer)*

The Seder Ritual

I. Kadeish (the blessings and the first cup of wine)

If the festival falls on a Friday night, the following is added:
And God saw everything that he had made, and behold, it was very good. And there was evening and there was morning, a sixth day. Thus the heavens and the earth were finished, and all the host of them. And on the seventh day God finished his work which he had done, and he rested on the seventh day from all his work which he had done. So God blessed the seventh day and hallowed it, because on it God rested from all his work which he had done in creation. [Genesis 1:31–2:3]

On weekdays start here (the words in parentheses and underlined are used for Friday night services only):
Blessed are you, O Lord, our God, King of the Universe, creator of the fruit of the vine.

Blessed are you, O Lord, our God, King of the Universe, who selected us from among all people and exalted us from among nations, and sanctified us with his commandments. And you, O Lord, our God, have given us (<u>Sabbath days for rest and</u>) festival days for joy, (<u>this Sabbath and the day of</u>) this feast of the unleavened bread, the time of our deliverance (<u>in love</u>) in remembrance of the departure from Egypt. For you selected us and sanctified us from among all nations, and caused us to inherit your holy

✡ 1 †

(<u>Sabbath and</u>) festival days (<u>in love and favor</u>). Blessed are you, O Lord, who hallows (<u>the Sabbath and</u>) Israel and the festival days.

If the festival falls on a Saturday night, add the following two paragraphs:

Blessed are you, O Lord, our God, King of the Universe, creator of the radiance of the fire.

Blessed are you, O Lord, Our God, King of the Universe, who has made a distinction between holy and unholy, between light and darkness, between Israel and all other nations, between the seventh day and the six working days. You discriminated between the sanctity of the Sabbath day and the sacredness of the festival; and you consecrated the seventh day in preference to the six working days; you separated your people Israel and sanctified them with your holiness. Blessed are you, O Lord, who makes the distinction between holy and unholy [as for this last line: cf. Leviticus 10:10: "You are to distinguish between the holy and the common, and between the unclean and the clean"].

All nights conclude:

Blessed are you, O Lord, Our God, King of the Universe, who has preserved us alive, sustained us, and brought us to enjoy this season.

<small>DRINK THE FIRST CUP OF WINE IN A RECLINING
POSITION (ALL WINE IS DRUNK RECLINING).</small>
The first cup drunk at the seder is the kiddush cup (the cup of sanctification), for blessing the festival day; the second cup (judgment) introduces Psalm 113.[1] The third

[1] See pp. 20–21 for Psalm 113.

cup (redemption) is taken just after the meal of the un-leavened bread. *The fourth cup (Kingdom) is used in singing Psalms 115–118 and for the final prayer and ex-hortation (see below). This tradition of four comes from the four promises that God made in Exodus: I will bring, I will rid, I will redeem, and I will take.*[2]

II. Ur'chatz *(washing the hands)*

WASH THE HANDS (AT LEAST THE LEADER DOES SO, BUT ALL MAY DO SO).

III. Karpas *(appetizer)*

THE LEADER THEN TAKES SOME KARPAS, DIPS IT
IN SALT WATER, AND DISTRIBUTES IT TO
ALL PRESENT, SAYING:

Blessed are you, O Lord, Our God, King of the Universe, creator of the fruits of the earth.

בָּרוּךְ אַתָּה יְיָ אֱלֹהֵינוּ מֶלֶךְ הָעוֹלָם בּוֹרֵא פְּרִי הַגָּפֶן:

BAW-RUCH A-TAW A-DO-NOI EL-O-HA-NU ME-LECH HAW-O-LAWM BO-RAY P'-REE HA-GAW-FEN.

ALL EAT THE KARPAS.

IV. Yachatz *(breaking the middle matzah)*

THE LEADER THEN TAKES THE COVERED MATZAH,
BREAKS THE MIDDLE MATZAH IN TWO, LEAVING

_____

[2] "Wherefore say unto the children of Israel, I am the LORD, and I will bring you out from under the burdens of the Egyptians, and I will rid you out of their bondage, and I will redeem you with a stretched out arm, and with great judgments: And I will take you to me for a people, and I will be to you a God: and ye shall know that I am the LORD your God, which bringeth you out from under the burdens of the Egyptians." [Exodus 6:6–7]

✿ 3 ✝

ONE HALF BETWEEN THE TWO WHOLE ONES AND PUTTING THE OTHER HALF UNDER A CLOTH FOR THE "AFIKOMEN," WHICH IS EATEN AT THE CONCLUSION OF THE PASSOVER FEAST. THEN HE ELEVATES THE DISH OF MATZAH, AND ALL (OR AS MANY AS CAN) SEATED AT THE TABLE TAKE HOLD AND SAY:

V. Magid *(the telling)*
1. Ha Lachma Anya *(invitation to the seder)*

This is the bread of affliction which our ancestors ate in the land of Egypt; let all who are hungry, enter and eat; and all who are in distress, come and celebrate the Passover. At present we celebrate it here, but next year we hope to celebrate it in the land of Israel. This year we are servants here, but next year we hope to be free in the land of Israel.

V. Magid *(the telling)*
2. Mah Nistanah *(The Four Questions)*

THE PLATE IS PUT DOWN AND THE SECOND CUP OF WINE IS FILLED. THEN THE YOUNGEST PRESENT ASKS THE FOUR QUESTIONS.

Reciting the Four Questions is the most famous part of the service, and it is said by a child. The seder itself is geared to families and, especially, the teaching function of parents to children. Exodus 12:26–27[3] enjoins parents to answer their child's query about the meaning of the service. Please note that the way the Four Questions are usually presented, there is really one question with four

---

[3] "And when your children say to you, 'What do you mean by this service?' you shall say, 'It is the sacrifice of the LORD's passover, for he passed over the houses of the people of Israel in Egypt, when he slew the Egyptians but spared our houses.'" [Exodus 12:26–27]

answers, though some translations revise it to present the four explanations in question form. The rest of the seder may be said to be an extended explanation bearing on these questions.

Why is this night different from all other nights?

On all other nights we may eat either leavened or unleavened bread, but on this night only unleavened bread.

On all other nights we may eat any type of herbs, but on this night only bitter herbs.

On all other nights we do not dip our bread even once, but on this night twice.

On all other nights we eat and drink either sitting or reclined, but on this night reclined.[4]

מַה נִּשְׁתַּנָּה הַלַּיְלָה הַזֶּה מִכָּל הַלֵּילוֹת:

שֶׁבְּכָל הַלֵּילוֹת אָנוּ אוֹכְלִין חָמֵץ וּמַצָּה. הַלַּיְלָה הַזֶּה כֻּלוֹ מַצָּה:

שֶׁבְּכָל הַלֵּילוֹת אָנוּ אוֹכְלִין שְׁאָר יְרָקוֹת. הַלַּיְלָה הַזֶּה מָרוֹר:

שֶׁבְּכָל הַלֵּילוֹת אֵין אָנוּ מַטְבִּילִין אֲפִילוּ פַּעַם אֶחָת. הַלַּיְלָה הַזֶּה שְׁתֵּי פְעָמִים:

שֶׁבְּכָל הַלֵּילוֹת אָנוּ אוֹכְלִין בֵּין יוֹשְׁבִין וּבֵין מְסֻבִּין. הַלַּיְלָה הַזֶּה כֻּלָּנוּ מְסֻבִּין:

---

[4] The Haggadah itself does not explain adequately *why* we should recline, so this footnote will have to suffice. In the ancient Middle East, only free men reclined at table while the Hebrews, then slaves, stood. The fact that after the exodus they were no longer slaves, but freed by the blood of the lamb (which, obviously, took on a more dramatic meaning after Christ's Passion), is indicated by their ritually reclining. A very interesting side-note: In John 13:1–2 and John 21:20, Jesus leaned on John to demonstrate the freedom from Egyptian slavery, wrought through the original lamb sacrifice at the Passover.

MA NISH-TA-NAW HA-LAIL-LAW HA-ZEH MEE-KAWL HA-LAY-LOS?

SHE-B'CHAWL HA-LAY-LOS AW-NU O-CH'LEEN CHAW-MAYTZ U-MA-TZAW, HA-LAI-LAW HA-ZEH KU-LO MA-TZAW.

SHE-B'CHAWL HA-LAY-LOS AW-NU O-CH'LEEN SH'AWR Y'RAW-KOS, HA-LAI-LAW HA-ZEH MAW-ROR.

SHE-B'CHAWL HA-LAY-LOS AYN AW-NU MAIT-BEE-LEEN A-FEE-LU PA-AM E-CHOS, HA-LAI-LAW HA-ZEH SH'TAY F'AW-MEEM.

SHE-B'CHAWL HA-LAY-LOS AW-NU O-CH'LEEN BAYN YO-SH'VEEN U-VAYN M'SU-BEEN, HA-LAI-LAW HA-ZEH KU-LAW-NU M'SU-BEEN.

THE DISH OF MATZAH IS REPLACED ON THE TABLE, AND THE LEADER OR MEMBERS OF THE COMPANY RESPOND:

Here is the explanation why the seder is celebrated: Because we were slaves to Pharaoh in Egypt, and the Lord, our God, brought us forth with a mighty hand and an outstretched arm. And if the Most Holy, blessed be he, had not brought forth our ancestors from Egypt, we and our children and our children's children would still be in bondage to the Pharaohs in Egypt. Therefore, even if we were all of us wise, all of us learned in the Law, it nevertheless would be incumbent upon us to speak of the departure from Egypt, and all who do so are accounted praiseworthy.

And it is related of Rabbi Eliezer, Rabbi Joshua, Rabbi Elazar the son of Azariah, Rabbi Akivah, and Rabbi Tarphon that they once met (on the night of Passover) in Bene-Berak and spoke of the departure from Egypt all that night, until their disciples came, and said thus: "Masters, the time has come to read the morning sh'ma."[5]

Rabbi Elazar the son of Azariah said, "In truth, I am like a man of seventy, yet I was not able to prove that the narration of the departure of Egypt should be made at night, until the son of Zoma proved it from the following words of scripture: 'that all the days of your life you may remember the day when you came out of the land of Egypt.'" [Deuteronomy 16:3] "The days of your life," the son of Zoma said, refers to the days alone, but "*all* the days of your life" include the nights also. The doctors, however, say, "the days of your life" refers to this world only, but "*all* the days of your life" include the time of the Messiah.

V. *Magid* (the telling)
3. *The Four Sons*

The seder is meant to be a family celebration, and the head of the household is supposed to relate the teachings to the younger generation, who are encouraged to participate fully in the service. Here the Haggadah speaks of four different sons and their questions about the seder. The wise son seeks knowledge, the wicked son mocks his parents, the simple son asks simple questions, and the son unable to ask needs to be instructed.

[5] The sh'ma is said twice daily by observant Jews ("when you lie down, and when you rise"), and it is the prayer put inside *mezuzahs* on doorposts of homes and inside *tefillin*, sets of small cubic leather boxes painted black containing scrolls, worn on the arm and around the head for ritual prayer. Here is the full prayer: "Hear, O Israel: The LORD our God is one LORD; and you shall love the LORD your God with all your heart, and with all your soul, and with all your might. And these words which I command you this day shall be upon your heart; and you shall teach them diligently to your children, and shall talk of them when you sit in your house, and when you walk by the way, and when you lie down, and when you rise. And you shall bind them as a sign upon your hand, and they shall be as frontlets between your eyes. And you shall write them on the doorposts of your house and on your gates." [Deuteronomy 6:4–9]

Blessed be God, blessed be he who has given the Law to his people Israel. Blessed be he whose Law speaks distinctly of the four different characters of children: the wise, the wicked, the simple, and the one without the capacity to inquire.

What says the wise son? He asks, "What is the meaning of the testimonies and the statutes and the ordinances which the LORD our God has commanded you?" [Deuteronomy 6:20] Then you shall instruct him in the laws of Passover, teaching him that after the paschal lamb no dessert ought to be set on the table.

What says the wicked son? He asks, "What do you mean by this service?" [Exodus 12:26] By the word "you," he indicates that he does not include himself and has withdrawn from the community. It is therefore proper to retort him by saying, "It is because of what the LORD did for me when I came out of Egypt" [Exodus 13:8]; for me and not for him, for had he been there, he would not have been thought worthy to be redeemed.

What says the simple son? He asks: "What is this?" Then you shall tell him: "By strength of hand the LORD brought us out of Egypt, from the house of bondage." [Exodus 13:14; see also Deuteronomy 5:15; 6:21, 7:8, 7:19, 9:26, 11:2, 26:8, 34:12; Daniel 9:15, among many such passages]

But as for him who has no capacity to inquire, you must begin the narration as it is said: "And you shall tell your son on that day, 'It is because of what the LORD did for me when I came out of Egypt.'" [Exodus 13:8]

✡ 8 ✝

One might possibly think that the narration was given from the first day of the month of Nissan; therefore it is said, "on that day." Yet, as it is said on that day, it might be inferred that day-time only was meant. But scripture says "on account of this," from which it can be inferred that the narration is to be made only at a time when the unleavened bread and bitter herbs are placed before you.

Now an explanation of how the Hebrew people ended up in Egypt. It starts with the notion that, prior to Abraham, who is the original father of the Jewish people, they were sinners, idolators.

Originally our ancestors were idolators, but at present the Lord has brought us near to his service; as it is said, "And Joshua said to all the people, 'Thus says the LORD, the God of Israel, "Your fathers lived of old beyond the Euphra'tes, Terah, the father of Abraham and of Nahor; and they served other gods. Then I took your father Abraham from beyond the River and led him through all the land of Canaan, and made his offspring many. I gave him Isaac; and to Isaac I gave Jacob and Esau. And I gave Esau the hill country of Se'ir to possess, but Jacob and his children went down to Egypt.""" [Joshua 24:2–4; see also Genesis 11:24–32[6]]

---

[6] "When Nahor had lived twenty-nine years, he became the father of Terah; and Nahor lived after the birth of Terah a hundred and nineteen years, and had other sons and daughters. When Terah had lived seventy years, he became the father of Abram, Nahor, and Haran. Now these are the descendants of Terah. Terah was the father of Abram, Nahor, and Haran; and Haran was the father of Lot. Haran died before his father Terah in the land of his birth, in Ur of the Chalde'ans. And Abram and Nahor took wives; the name of Abram's wife was Sar'ai, and the name of Nahor's wife, Milcah, the daughter of Haran the father of Milcah and Iscah. Now Sar'ai was barren; she had no child. Terah took Abram his son and Lot the son of Haran, his grandson, and Sar'ai his daugh-ter-in-law, his son Abram's wife, and they went forth together from Ur of the Chalde'ans to go into the land of Canaan; but when they

I. Kadeish
(blessings and first cup of wine)
II. Ur'chatz
(washing the hands)
III. Karpas
(appetizer)
IV. Yachatz
(breaking the middle matzah)
V. Magid
(the telling)
1. Ha Lachma Anya
(invitation to seder)
2. Ma Nistanah
(The Four Questions)
3. The Four Sons
4. "Go and learn"
5. Kos Sheini
(second cup of wine)
VI. Rohtzah
(ritual wash-ing of hands)
VII. Motzi
("who brings forth")
VIII. Matzo
(blessing of the matzah)
IX. Maror
(bitter herbs)
X. Koreich
(the Hillel sandwich)
XI. Shulchan Orech
(the meal)
XII. Tzafun
(eating the afikomen)
XIII. Boreich
(grace after meals)
1. Kos Shlishi
(the third cup of wine)
2. Kos shel Eliyahu ha-Navi (Cup of Elijah)
XIV. Hallel
(songs of praise)
XV. Nirtzah
(concluding song and prayer)

Blessed be he, who observes strictly his promise to Israel. Blessed be the Most Holy, who computed the end of the captivity, that he might perform what he had promised to our father Abraham at the covenant between them, as it is said, "Then the LORD said to Abram, 'Know of a surety that your descendants will be sojourners in a land that is not theirs, and will be slaves there, and they will be oppressed for four hundred years; but I will bring judgment on the nation which they serve, and afterward they shall come out with great possessions.'" [Genesis 15: 13–14]

ELEVATE THE CUP OF WINE AND SAY:

And it is that promise which has been the support of our ancestors and of ourselves, for not one only has risen up against us, but in every generation some have arisen against us to annihilate us, but the Most Holy, blessed be he, has always delivered us out of their hands.

V. Magid (the telling)
4. "Go and learn"

PUT THE CUP DOWN.

The Haggadah now expounds on the four verses in Deuteronomy 26:5–8,[7] starting with a short introduction

came to Haran, they settled there. The days of Terah were two hundred and five years; and Terah died in Haran." [Genesis 11:24–32; cf. also Genesis 33, Deuteronomy 2:5, and Genesis 46:5–7.]

[7] The full reading goes as follows: "And you shall make response before the LORD your God, 'A wandering Aramean [sometimes "Syrian"] was my father; and he went down into Egypt and sojourned there, few in number; and there he became a nation, great, mighty, and populous. And the Egyptians treated us harshly, and afflicted us, and laid upon us hard bondage. Then we cried to the LORD the God of our fathers, and the LORD heard our voice,

of Laban. Each verse is then explained clause by clause; the clause in question is written in boldface.

The first verse

Go forth and inquire what Laban, the Syrian, intended to do to our father Jacob. Pharaoh decreed the destruction of the males only, while Laban designed to root out the whole, as it is said, "And you shall make response before the LORD your God, 'A wandering Aramean [sometimes "Syrian"] was my father; and he went down into Egypt and sojourned there, few in number; and there he became a nation, great, mighty, and populous.'" [Deuteronomy 26:5[8]]

And he went down into Egypt: compelled by the word of God; **and sojourned there:** by which we are taught that he did not go down to settle, but only to sojourn, as it is said: "They said to Pharaoh, 'We have come to sojourn in the land; for there is no pasture for your servants' flocks, for the famine is severe in the land of Canaan; and now, we pray you, let your servants dwell in the land of Goshen.'" [Genesis 47:4]

and saw our affliction, our toil, and our oppression; and the LORD brought us out of Egypt with a mighty hand and an outstretched arm, with great terror, with signs and wonders.'" [Deuteronomy 26:5–8]

[8] This refers to Jacob's father-in-law Laban, father of Leah and Rachel, Jacob's wives. Laban was also the brother of Rebecca, the wife of Isaac and the granddaughter of Nahor, the brother of Abraham. Laban deceived Jacob, who had worked for him for seven years as payment for allowing him to marry Rachel, the younger sister. When the time came to consummate the marriage, Laban surreptitiously sent in Leah. The next day, when Jacob complained, Laban gave him Rachel also, but only after he agreed to another seven years of work. Laban sought to keep Jacob and his wives, children, and servants on his land, but Jacob finally left after a bit of deception on his part. Thus it can be said that Laban sought to get between the promise that God had given Jacob's grandfather Abraham and reaffirmed with him to be the father of nations.

Few in number: as it is said: "Your fathers went down to Egypt seventy persons; and now the LORD your God has made you as the stars of heaven for multitude." [Deuteronomy 10:22; cf. Deuteronomy 1:10: "the LORD your God has multiplied you, and behold, you are this day as the stars of heaven for multitude"; cf. also Genesis 46:27: ". . . all the persons of the house of Jacob, that came into Egypt, were seventy."] **And there he became a nation**: by which we are taught that the children of Israel were distinguished even in Egypt. **Great, mighty**: as it is said: "But the descendants of Israel were fruitful and increased greatly; they multiplied and grew exceedingly strong; so that the land was filled with them." [Exodus 1:7] **And populous**: as it is said: "I said to you in your blood, 'Live, and grow up like a plant of the field.' And you grew up and became tall and arrived at full maidenhood; your breasts were formed, and your hair had grown; yet you were naked and bare."[Ezekiel 16:6–7]

The second verse
"And the Egyptians treated us harshly, and afflicted us, and laid upon us hard bondage." [Deuteronomy 26:6]

And the Egyptian treated us harshly: as it is said, "Come, let us deal shrewdly with them, lest they multiply, and, if war befall us, they join our enemies and fight against us and escape from the land." [Exodus 1:10] **And afflicted us**: as it is said, "they set taskmasters over them to afflict them with heavy burdens; and they built for Pharaoh store-cities, Pithom and Ra-am'ses." [Exodus 1:11] **And laid upon us heavy bondage**: as it is said, "So they [the Egyptians] made the people of Israel serve with rigor." [Exodus 1:13]

The third verse

"Then we cried to the LORD the God of our fathers, and the LORD heard our voice, and saw our affliction, our toil, and our oppression." [cf. Deuteronomy 26:7]

Then we cried to the LORD, the God of our fathers: as it is said, "In the course of those many days the king of Egypt died. And the people of Israel groaned under their bondage, and cried out for help, and their cry under bondage came up to God." [Exodus 2:23] **And the LORD heard our voice:** as it is said, "And God heard their groaning, and God remembered his covenant with Abraham, with Isaac, and with Jacob." [Exodus 2:24] **Saw our affliction:** this denotes the separation from their wives, as it is said, "And God saw the people of Israel, and God knew their condition." [Exodus 2:25] **Our toil:** this denotes the destruction of the male children, as it is said, "Every son that is born to the Hebrews you shall cast into the Nile, but you shall let every daughter live." [Exodus 1:22] **And our oppression:** this denotes the severity employed, as it is said, "and I have seen the oppression with which the Egyptians oppress them." [Exodus 3:9]

The fourth, and last, verse

"And the LORD brought us out of Egypt with a mighty hand and an outstretched arm, with great terror, with signs and wonders." [Deuteronomy 26:8]

And the Lord brought us out of Egypt: not by means of an angel, nor by means of a Seraph, nor by means of a messenger; but the most Holy, blessed be he, in his own glory, as it is said: "For I will pass through the land of Egypt that night, and I will smite all the first-born in the land of Egypt, both man and beast; and on all the gods of Egypt I will execute judgments: I am the LORD. [Exodus 12:12]

Now a clause-by-clause explanation from the passage in Exodus:

For I will pass through the land of Egypt that night: I myself and not an angel. *And I will smite all the first-born in the land of Egypt, both man and beast*: I myself and not a seraph: **And on all the gods of Egypt I will execute judgments**: I myself and not a messenger. **I am the Lord**: I am he, and none other.

Back to the clause-by-clause explanation from above.

With a mighty hand: this refers to the pestilence, as it is said, "Behold, the hand of the LORD will fall with a very severe plague upon your cattle which are in the field, the horses, the asses, the camels, the herds, and the flocks" [Exodus 9:3] **And an outstretched arm**: this refers to the sword, as it is said, "and in his hand a drawn sword stretched out over Jerusalem." [1 Chronicles 21:16] **With great terror**: this refers to the appearance of the Divine Presence, as it is said, "Or has any god ever attempted to go and take a nation for himself from the midst of another nation, by trials, by signs, by wonders, and by war, by a mighty hand and an outstretched arm, and by great terrors, according to all that the LORD your God did for you in Egypt before your eyes?" [Deuteronomy 4:34] **With signs**, this refers to the rod with which the miracles were performed, as it is said, "And you shall take in your hand this rod, with which you shall do the signs." [Exodus 4:17] **And wonders**, this refers to the plague of blood, as it is said, "And I will give portents in the heavens and on the earth, blood and fire and columns of smoke." [Joel 2:30]

Another explanation is thus: with a strong hand denotes two plagues, with an outstretched arm, two more, with great terror, two more, with signs, two more, and with wonders, two more. – These are the ten plagues which the Most Holy, blessed be he, brought upon the Egyptians in Egypt, viz.: –

It is traditional to dip your finger in the cup of wine and shake off one drop at a time at the mention of each of the ten plagues visited upon the Egyptians. These plagues are explained in Exodus 7:15–12:33, each representing a pagan deity.

> blood
> frogs
> vermin
> wild beasts
> pestilence
> boils
> hail
> locusts
> darkness, and
> the slaying of the first-born

The learned rabbis indicate that these plagues were not the only, or even the worst, that the Egyptians suffered.

Rabbi Jose, the Galilean, said: When can you assert that the Egyptians were smitten with ten plagues in Egypt, and in the Red Sea they were smitten with fifty plagues? He answered thus: Of Egypt, it is said, "And the magicians said to Pharaoh, 'This is the finger of God.'" [Exodus 8:19] But of the sea, it is said, "And Israel saw the great work which the LORD did against the Egyptians, and the people feared the LORD; and they believed in the LORD and in his servant Moses." [Exodus 14:31] If by the finger only they were smitten with ten plagues in Egypt, it may be deduced that in the Red Sea they were smitten with fifty plagues.

I. Kadeish (blessings and first cup of wine)
II. Ur'chatz (washing the hands)
III. Karpas (appetizer)
IV. Yachatz (breaking the middle matzah)
V. Magid (the telling)
1. Ha Lachma Anya (invitation to seder)
2. Ma Nistanah (The Four Questions)
3. The Four Sons
4. "Go and learn"
5. Kos Sheini (second cup of wine)
VI. Rohtzah (ritual washing of hands)
VII. Motzi ("who brings forth")
VIII. Matzo (blessing of the matzah)
IX. Maror (bitter herbs)
X. Koreich (the Hillel sandwich)
XI. Shulchan Orech (the meal)
XII. Tzafun (eating the afikomen)
XIII. Boreich (grace after meals)
1. Kos Shlishi (the third cup of wine)
2. Kos shel Eliyahu ha-Navi (Cup of Elijah)
XIV. Hallel (songs of praise)
XV. Nirtzah (concluding song and prayer)

Rabbi Eleazar said: Where can it be deduced that every plague which the Most Holy, blessed be he, brought upon the Egyptians in Egypt consisted of four different plagues? Because it is said, "He let loose on them his fierce anger, / wrath, indignation, and distress, / a company of destroying angels. [Psalms 78:49] Wrath is one, Indignation two, Distress three, and a company of destroying angels four. Hence it may be deduced that while in Egypt they were smitten with forty plagues, in the Red Sea they were smitten with two hundred plagues.

Rabbi Akivah said: Where can it be deduced that each plague which the Most Holy, blessed be he, brought upon the Egyptians in Egypt consisted of the five plagues? Because it is said, "He let loose on them his fierce anger, / wrath, indignation, and distress, / a company of destroying angels. [Psalms 78:49] His Fierce anger is one, Wrath is two, Indignation three, Distress four, and a company of destroying angels is five. Hence it may be deduced that while in Egypt they were smitten with fifty plagues, in the Red Sea they were smitten with two hundred and fifty plagues.

How many abundant favors has the Lord performed upon us.

Here it is traditional to recite prayers of praise for the deliverance of the Hebrew people. These prayers are sung and either build one upon the other (like the "Twelve Days of Christmas") or repeat a refrain.

The most famous of these songs is Dayeinu (die ay' new, which means, "it would have been sufficient," which is the refrain after each of the fifteen stanzas). It speaks of the overabundance of God in giving the Hebrew people freedom and life, shown in the fifteen gifts below:

Five Stanzas of Leaving Slavery

   1. If he had brought us out of Egypt.
   2. If he had executed justice upon the Egyptians.
   3. If he had executed justice upon their gods.
   4. If he had slain their first born.
   5. If he had given to us their health and wealth.

Five Stanzas of Miracles

6. If he had split the sea for us.

7. If he had led us through on dry land.

8. If he had drowned our oppressors.

9. If he had provided for our needs in the wilderness for 40 years.

10. If he had fed us manna.

Five Stanzas of Being with God

11. If he had given us Shabbat.

12. If he had led us to Mount Sinai.

13. If he had given us the Torah.

14. If he had brought us into the Land of Israel.

15. If he had built the Temple for us.

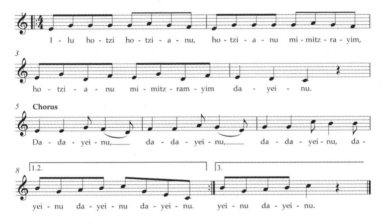

Here is the first half of the first stanza in Hebrew. That first full stanza in English is:

"If he had brought us forth from Egypt, and had not inflicted judgment upon the Egyptians, it would have been sufficient."

Transliterated, the first half stanza is ilu hotzianu mimitzrayim . . . dayeinu, *and is sung thus:*

ilu hotzi

hotzianu

hotzianu

mimitzrayim

hotzianu

mimitzrayim

dayeinu

refrain:

day day einu

day day einu

day day einu

dayeinu dayeinu dayeinu

(repeat)

A summation thus far

How much more are we indebted for the manifold bounties which the Omnipresent has bestowed upon us. He brought us forth from Egypt, executed judgment upon the Egyptians and their gods, slew their first-born, gave us their wealth, divided the sea for us, caused us to pass through its midst on dry land, drowned our adversaries in the sea, supplied us with everything during forty years, fed us with manna, gave us the Sabbath, led us to Mount Sinai, gave us the Law, brought us to the land of Israel, and built the holy temple for us to atone for our iniquities.

Rabbi Gamliel said that whoever does not make mention of the three things at the Passover feast has not done his duty, namely, the sacrifice of the Passover, the unleavened bread, and the bitter herbs.

This section of the Haggadah concludes with an explanation of these matters and the symbolism of the ceremonial foods.

Pointing to the lamb shank: The Paschal lamb, which our ancestors ate during the existence of the Temple, for what reason was it eaten? Because the Omnipresent, blessed be he, passed over the houses of our ancestors in Egypt, as it is said, "you shall say, 'It is the sacrifice of the LORD's passover, for he passed over the houses of the people of Israel in Egypt, when he slew the Egyptians but spared our houses.' And the people bowed their heads and worshiped." [Exodus 12:27]

Pointing to the matzah: This unleavened bread which we now eat, what does it mean? It is eaten because the dough of our ancestors had not time to become leavened before the supreme King of kings, the Most Holy, blessed be he, revealed himself to them and redeemed them, as it is said: "And they baked unleavened cakes of the dough which they had brought out of Egypt, for it was not leavened, because they were thrust out of Egypt and could not tarry, neither had they prepared for themselves any provisions." [Exodus 12:39]

Pointing to the bitter herbs: This bitter herb which we eat, what does it mean?[9] It is eaten because the Egyptians embittered the lives of our ancestors in Egypt, as it is said: They "made their lives bitter with hard service, in mortar and brick, and in all kinds of work in the field; in all their work they made them serve with rigor." [Exodus 1:14]

In every generation each individual is bound to regard himself as if he had personally gone forth from Egypt, as it is said: "And you shall tell your son on that day, 'It is because of what the LORD did for me when I came out of Egypt.'" [Exodus 13:8] Thus it was not our ancestors alone, whom the Most Holy, blessed be he, then redeemed but us also did he

---

[9] Judaism commands that enough maror be eaten "to bring tears to the eyes." It is interesting to note that at the moment Jesus identified his betrayer ("He who has dipped his hand in the dish with me, will betray me." [Matthew 26:23]), the ritual prescribed that all at the table be crying. It was a mournful moment, prophesied in Psalm 41:9: "Even my bosom friend in whom I trusted, who ate of my bread, has lifted his heel against me."

I. Kadeish (blessings and first cup of wine)

II. Ur'chatz (washing the hands)

III. Karpas (appetizer)

IV. Yachatz (breaking the middle matzah)

V. Magid (the telling)

1. Ha Lachma Anya (invitation to seder)

2. Ma Nistanah (The Four Questions)

3. The Four Sons

4. "Go and learn"

5. Kos Sheini (second cup of wine)

VI. Rohtzah (ritual washing of hands)

VII. Motzi ("who brings forth")

VIII. Matzo (blessing of the matzah)

IX. Maror (bitter herbs)

X. Koreich (the Hillel sandwich)

XI. Shulchan Orech (the meal)

XII. Tzafun (eating the afikomen)

XIII. Boreich (grace after meals)

1. Kos Shlishi (the third cup of wine)

2. Kos shel Eliyahu ha-Navi (Cup of Elijah)

XIV. Hallel (songs of praise)

XV. Nirtzah (concluding song and prayer)

redeem with them, as it is said: "and he brought us out from there, that he might bring us in and give us the land which he swore to give to our fathers." [Deuteronomy 6:23]

V. Magid *(the telling)*
5. Kos Sheini *(second cup of wine)*

ELEVATE THE CUP OF WINE AND SAY:

Therefore, we are bound to thank, praise, laud, glorify, extol, honor, bless, exalt, and reverence him who performed for our father and for us all these miracles. He brought us from slavery to freedom, from sorrow to joy, from mourning to festivity, and from servitude to redemption. Let us therefore sing a new song in his presence. Hallelujah!

PUT THE CUP DOWN AND READ (PERHAPS RESPONSIVELY) PSALMS 113 AND 114:

Praise the LORD!
Praise, O servants of the LORD,
praise the name of the LORD!
Blessed be the name of the LORD
from this time forth and for evermore!
From the rising of the sun to its setting
the name of the LORD is to be praised!
The LORD is high above all nations,
and his glory above the heavens!
Who is like the LORD our God,
who is seated on high,
who looks far down
upon the heavens and the earth?
He raises the poor from the dust,
and lifts the needy from the ash heap,

I. Kadeish (blessings and first cup of wine)
II. Ur'chatz (washing the hands)
III. Karpas (appetizer)
IV. Yachatz (breaking the middle matzah)
V. Magid (the telling)
  1. Ha Lachma Anya (invitation to seder)
  2. Ma Nistanah (The Four Questions)
  3. The Four Sons
  4. "Go and learn"
  5. Kos Sheini (second cup of wine)
VI. Rohtzah (ritual washing of hands)
VII. Motzi ("who brings forth")
VIII. Matzo (blessing of the matzah)
IX. Maror (bitter herbs)
X. Koreich (the Hillel sandwich)
XI. Shulchan Orech (the meal)
XII. Tzafun (eating the afikomen)
XIII. Boreich (grace after meals)
  1. Kos Shlishi (the third cup of wine)
  2. Kos shel Eliyahu ha-Navi (Cup of Elijah)
XIV. Hallel (songs of praise)
XV. Nirtzah (concluding song and prayer)

to make them sit with princes,
with the princes of his people.
He gives the barren woman a home,
making her the joyous mother of children.
Praise the LORD! [Psalm 113]

When Israel went forth from Egypt,
the house of Jacob from a people of strange language,
Judah became his sanctuary,
Israel his dominion.
The sea looked and fled,
Jordan turned back.
The mountains skipped like rams,
the hills like lambs.
What ails you, O sea, that you flee?
O Jordan, that you turn back?
O mountains, that you skip like rams?
O hills, like lambs?
Tremble, O earth, at the presence of the LORD,
at the presence of the God of Jacob,
who turns the rock into a pool of water,
the flint into a spring of water. [Psalm 114]

ELEVATE THE CUP OF WINE AND SAY:

Blessed are you, O Lord our God, King of the universe, who has redeemed us and our ancestors from Egypt and has brought us to the enjoyment of this night, to eat unleavened bread and bitter herbs. You, O Lord our God, and God of our ancestors, may you bring us to enjoy in peace other solemn feasts and sacred seasons, which approach us, that we may rejoice in the building of your city and exult in your holy service, that we may there eat of the sacrifices and of the holy paschal offerings, whose blood shall

✡ 21 †

be sprinkled upon the side of your altar, for your acceptance. Then shall we, with a new hymn, give thanks to you for our deliverance, and for the redemption of our souls. Blessed are you, O Lord, who has redeemed Israel.

Blessed are you, O Lord our God, creator of the fruit of the vine.

בָּרוּךְ אַתָּה יְיָ אֱלֹהֵינוּ מֶלֶךְ הָעוֹלָם בּוֹרֵא פְּרִי הַגָּפֶן:

BAW-RUCH A-TAW A-DO-NOI EL-O-HA-NU ME-LECH HAW-O-LAWM BO-RAY P'-REE HA-GAW-FEN.

DRINK THE SECOND CUP OF WINE.

VI. Rohtzah (ritual washing of hands)

WASH THE HANDS[10] AND SAY:

Blessed are you, O Lord our God, King of the universe, who has sanctified us with your commandments and commanded us to wash the hands.

בָּרוּךְ אַתָּה יְיָ אֱלֹהֵינוּ מֶלֶךְ הָעוֹלָם אֲשֶׁר קִדְּשָׁנוּ
בְּמִצְוֹתָיו וְצִוָּנוּ עַל נְטִילַת יָדָיִם:

BAW-RUCH A-TAW A-DO-NOI EL-O-HA-NU ME-LECH HAW-O-LAWM A-SHER KID-D'SHAW-NU B'MITZ-VO-SAWV V'TZEE-VAW-NU AL N'TEE-LAS YAW-DAW-YEEM.

VII. Motzi ("who brings forth")

THE LEADER TAKES THE TWO WHOLE MATZAHS

---

[10] It may well have been soon after this second hand-washing that Jesus, in another ironic twist on the seder ritual, washed the feet of his disciples. John 13:2 recounts that it was "during supper, when the devil had already put it into the heart of Judas Iscariot, Simon's son, to betray him."

AND THE BROKEN HALF AND SAYS THE
FOLLOWING BLESSING:

Blessed are you, O Lord our God, King of the Universe, who brings forth bread from the earth.

בָּרוּךְ אַתָּה יְיָ אֱלֹהֵינוּ מֶלֶךְ הָעוֹלָם הַמּוֹצִיא לֶחֶם מִן הָאָרֶץ:

BAW-RUCH A-TAW A-DO-NOI EL-O-HA-NU ME-LECH HAW-O-LAWM HA-MO-TZEE LE-CHEM MEEN HAW-AW-RETZ.

VIII. Matzo (blessing of the matzah)

Blessed are you, O Lord our God, King of the universe, who has sanctified us with your commandments, and commanded us to eat unleavened bread.

בָּרוּךְ אַתָּה יְיָ אֱלֹהֵינוּ מֶלֶךְ הָעוֹלָם אֲשֶׁר קִדְּשָׁנוּ בְּמִצְוֹתָיו וְצִוָּנוּ עַל אֲכִילַת מַצָּה:

BAW-RUCH A-TAW A-DO-NOI EL-O-HA-NU ME-LECH HAW-O-LAWM A-SHER KID-D'SHAW-NU B'MITZ-VO-SAWV V'TZEE-VAW-NU AL A-CHEE-LAS MA-TZAW.

IX. Maror (bitter herbs)

THE LEADER TAKES SOME BITTER HERBS, DIPS
THEM INTO CHAROSES AND SAYS:

Blessed are you, O Lord our God, King of the universe, who has sanctified us with your commandments and commanded us to eat bitter herbs.

בָּרוּךְ אַתָּה יְיָ אֱלֹהֵינוּ מֶלֶךְ הָעוֹלָם אֲשֶׁר קִדְּשָׁנוּ בְּמִצְוֹתָיו וְצִוָּנוּ עַל אֲכִילַת מָרוֹר:

BAW-RUCH A-TAW A-DO-NOI EL-O-HA-NU ME-LECH HAW-O-LAWM A-SHER KID-D'SHAW-NU B'MITZ-VO-SAWV V'TZEE-VAW-NU AL A-CHEE-LAS MAW-ROR.

X. Koreich (sandwich)

HE BREAKS THE BOTTOM PIECE OF MATZAH AND
DISTRIBUTES IT WITH SOME BITTER HERBS AND
CHAROSES TO MAKE THE "HILLEL SANDWICH,"
THEN SAYS:

Thus did Hillel during the existence of the holy temple: he took unleavened bread and bitter herbs, and
ate them together, in order to perform the Law. "With
unleavened bread and bitter herbs they shall eat it."
[Exodus 12:8][11]

EAT THE "SANDWICH."

XI. Shulchan Orech (the festive meal is served)

* * * * * * * *

XII. Tzafun (eating the afikomen)

AFTER SUPPER, THE HALF OF THE MIDDLE MATZAH
THAT HAD BEEN RESERVED EARLY IN THE SEDER,
CALLED THE *AFIKOMEN*,[12] IS DISTRIBUTED TO ALL
PRESENT AND EATEN. THEN THE THIRD CUP OF
WINE IS POURED. IF THE CUP OF ELIJAH HAS NOT
YET BEEN POURED, IT IS DONE SO NOW.

---

[11] One tradition cites the story of a young boy who asked Rabbi
Hillel, "Rabbi, why do we use such a sweet mixture to remember
such a bitter time?" The rabbi wisely replied, "My son, when redemption is nigh, even the bitterness of affliction is sweet."

[12] Let us to look more deeply into this interpretation of the
afikomen. The "matzah tash," the traditional pouch into which the
three pieces of matzah are placed, has three chambers, and it is
white, the symbol of holiness. Some traditions call it "echad,"
meaning "unity," the very word God uses to describe himself in the
sh'ma, "Hear, O Israel, the Lord our God is one Lord." It is interesting that in God's revelation of his oneness, he avoids the word

✡ 24 †

XIII. Boreich *(grace after meals)*[13]
Kos Shlishi *(the third cup of wine)*

On festive days, Psalm 126, which describes the joys of redemption, is often recited prior to the grace after meals.

When the LORD restored the fortunes of Zion,
we were like those who dream.
Then our mouth was filled with laughter,
and our tongue with shouts of joy;
then they said among the nations,
"The LORD has done great things for them."

"yachid," which refers to a singular, indivisible one, but uses "echad," which refers to a compound unity. So the tash consists of three pieces of unleavened matzah. The Talmud is replete with examples of leaven tied to sin, evil, and corruption. So we have the "holy unity" consisting of three unleavened entities. At one time during the service, not the first or the third, but only the second, of these unities is removed and broken. Part of it (the afikomen) goes back into the pouch, but part of it remains out in the world, is carefully wrapped in a shroud, is ritually buried somewhere in the room, only to be restored at the third cup, the cup of redemption. At that point the ancient prayer over bread is chanted, "Blessed are you, O Lord our God, King of the Universe, who brings forth bread from the earth." Jesus continually likened himself to bread [cf. Matthew 26:26, John 6:48, John 12:24] and was brought forth from the earth on the third day. According to Jewish legal codes, the bread must be unleavened (i.e., free of sin, evil, corruption), pierced and striped [see Isaiah 53:5: "But he was wounded for our transgressions, he was bruised for our iniquities; upon him was the chastisement that made us whole, and with his stripes we are healed."].

Strangely, during the period of the Second Temple (516 B.C. and 70 A.D.), the afikomen was the lamb itself. It was the focal point of the entire meal, eaten with great revelry as the symbol of freedom. But the ritual was changed from a lamb afikomen to a matzah afikomen. The reason may lie in history. No longer would Israel remember the death of an animal lamb, whose blood and body brought redemption for her ancestors in Egypt. Now Israel would focus on the new afikomen, the body of Jesus.

[13] Note that Jewish tradition has grace *after* the meal.

The LORD has done great things for us;
we are glad.
Restore our fortunes, O LORD,
like the watercourses in the Negeb!
May those who sow in tears
reap with shouts of joy!
He that goes forth weeping,
bearing the seed for sowing,
shall come home with shouts of joy,
bringing his sheaves with him. [Psalm 126]

Gentlemen, let us say grace: The name of the Lord be blessed from now unto eternity.

Let us bless him (*if in the company of ten or more, add:* <u>our God</u>), of whose gifts we have partaken.

Blessed be he (<u>our God</u>), of whose gifts we have partaken, and by whose goodness we exist.

Blessed be he, and blessed be his name!

Blessed are you, O Lord our God, King of the universe, who feeds the whole world with your goodness, and with grace, kindness, and mercy gives food to every creature, for his mercy endures forever. And as his abundant goodness has never been deficient toward us, so may we never be in want of sustenance forever and ever; for the sake of his great name for he is the God who feeds and sustains all, and deals beneficently with all; and provides food for all the creatures that he has created. Blessed are you, O Lord, who gives food for all.

We will give thanks to you, O Lord our God, for having caused our ancestors to inherit that desirable, good, and ample land; and because you have brought us forth from the land of Egypt, and redeemed us from the house of bondage; and for your covenant, which you have sealed in our flesh; for the law which you have taught us; and for your statutes which you have made known to us; and for the life, kindness, and mercy, which you have graciously bestowed on us; and for the food with which you feed and sustain us continually every day and hour.

And for all those things, O Lord our God, will we give thanks to you, and praise you. Blessed be your name continually, in the mouth of every living creature, forever and ever; as it is written, "And you shall eat and be full, and you shall bless the LORD your God for the good land he has given you." [Deuteronomy 8:10] Blessed are you, O Lord, for the gift of the land, and for the food.

O Lord our God, we beseech you, have compassion on your people Israel, on Jerusalem, your city, on Zion, the residence of your glory, on the kingdom of the house of David, your anointed; and on the great and holy house, which is called by your name. You are our God, Father, Pastor, and Feeder; our Maintainer, Supporter, and Deliverer. Deliver us speedily from all our troubles; and suffer us not, O Lord our God, to stand in need of the gifts of mankind, nor their loan, but let us depend on your full, open, holy, and extensive hand so that we may not be put to shame, not ever be confounded.

On the Sabbath say the following paragraph also:
Be pleased, O Lord our God, to grant us peace in your commandments, and in the commandment of the seventh day, even this great and holy Sabbath; for this day is great and holy in

your presence, a day to rest and be at ease, in love, according to the precept of your will; and in your good will, suffer no trouble, sorrow, or affliction, to affect us on our day of rest; and let us live to see, O Lord our God, the consolation of Zion, your city, and the rebuilding of Jerusalem, your holy city; for you are the Lord of salvation, and the Lord of consolation.

Our God and the God of our fathers, may you be pleased to grant that our remembrance and the remembrance of our fathers, the remembrance of the Messiah, the son of David, your servant, and the remembrance of Jerusalem, your holy city, and the remembrance of your people, the house of Israel, may ascend, come, approach, be seen, accepted, heard, and remembered for the granting of a happy deliverance, with favor, grace, mercy, life, and peace, on this day of Passover. O Lord our God, remember us this day for good, visit us with your blessing, and save us to enjoy life. And with the word of salvation and mercy, have compassion and be gracious to us. O have mercy upon us and save us, for our eyes are continually toward you, for you, O Lord, are a merciful and gracious King.

O build Jerusalem, the holy city, speedily in our days. Blessed are you, O Lord, who in your mercy builds Jerusalem. Amen.

Blessed are you, O Lord our God, King of the Universe. O God, you are our Father, King Almighty, Creator, Redeemer, and Sanctifier: the Sanctifier of Jacob, our Pastor, the Shepherd of Israel; the beneficent King, who deals beneficently toward us. He has dealt bountifully with us, as he does now, and ever will: granting us grace, favor, mercy, ease, deliverance, prosperity, blessing, salvation, consolation, maintenance, and sustenance, and a peaceable life and every good forever. And may we never lack any good thing.

May he who is most merciful reign over us forever and ever. May he who is most merciful be praised in heaven and on earth. May he who is most merciful be adored throughout all generations: be eternally glorified amidst us; and be honored among us, to all Eternity. May he who is most merciful maintain us with honor. May he who is most merciful break the yoke of our captivity from off our neck, and lead us securely to our land. May he who is most merciful send us abundant blessings in this house, and on this table on which we have eaten. May he who is most merciful send us Elijah, the prophet of blessed memory, to bring us the good tidings of salvation and consolation. May he is most merciful bless (*when sitting at a table other than that of one's parents, the underlined words in parentheses are to be omitted*) (<u>my honored father</u>), the head of this house; and (<u>my honored mother</u>), the mistress thereof; their house, their children, and all belonging to them. Bless us and all belonging to us. As our ancestors, Abraham, Isaac, and Jacob, were blessed with all and every good, bless us altogether with a complete blessing, and let us say, Amen.

May they in heaven show forth their and our merit, for a peaceable preservation, and may we receive à blessing from the Lord, and righteousness from the God of our salvation, and may we find grace and good understanding in the sight of God and man.

On the Sabbath, say the following sentence:
May he who is most merciful, cause us to inherit the day that is entirely Sabbath, and everlasting rest.

May he who is most merciful cause us to inherit the day that is entirely good.

May he who is most merciful make us worthy to behold the day of the Messiah and eternal life in the future state. He gives great salvation to his King, and shows mercy to his Anointed, to David and his seed forever. May he make peace in his high heavens; grant peace to us, and all Israel, and let us say, Amen.

Fear the Lord, you his saints, for there is no want to those who fear him. The young lions lack and suffer hunger, but they who seek the Lord shall not want any good. Praise you the Lord, for he is good; his mercy endures forever. You open your hand and satisfy the desire of every living thing. Blessed is the man who will trust in the Lord, and the Lord will be his trust.

I have been young and now I am old, yet have I not seen the righteous forsaken, nor his seed begging bread.

May the Lord give strength to his people. May the Lord bless his people with peace.

Blessed are you, O Lord our God, King of the Universe, creator of the fruit of the vine.

בָּרוּךְ אַתָּה יְיָ אֱלֹהֵינוּ מֶלֶךְ הָעוֹלָם בּוֹרֵא פְּרִי הַגָּפֶן:

BAW-RUCH A-TAW A-DO-NOI EL-O-HA-NU ME-LECH
HAW-O-LAWM BO-RAY P'-REE HA-GAW-FEN.

DRINK THE THIRD CUP OF WINE.

Very likely it was here, at the drinking of the third cup, the cup of redemption, that Jesus invoked the words that were certainly the most shocking ever heard by any of the disciples, "This is my body which is given for you. Do this in remembrance of me." [Luke 22:19] If we think of the prayers that have preceded this, concentrating on deliverance, remembrance, and thanksgiving (which together is the very meaning of "Eucharist"), perhaps we can appreciate the reaction that the disciples must have had. The 613 Laws in the Torah (the first five books of the Bible – Genesis, Exodus, Leviticus, Numbers, and Deuteronomy) emphasized purity, and here Jesus seems to be invoking the most horrific defilement of those laws of purity, cannibalism. In so doing, Jesus changes the meaning of deliverance from that of physical bondage to spiritual bondage, and places the Eucharist, his own Body, as the central remembrance for salvation, not that of the remembrance of the exodus. And, as the Haggadah makes clear, the Father is honored by our remembrance of our own exodus from Egypt, which is noted as "performing the Law," so Jesus asks us to remember him in our own victory in the Eucharist.

The Synoptic Gospels tie the prayer of bread to that of wine, when Jesus says, "Drink of it, all of you; for this is my blood of the covenant, which is poured out for many for the forgiveness of sins. I tell you I shall not drink again of this fruit of the vine until that day when I drink it new with you in my Father's kingdom." [Matthew 26:27–29] What seems to be clear is that the Last Supper participants never got to the obligatory fourth cup of wine (see below).

Finally, it must have been here, after the drinking of the third cup, that Jesus left the room and sought out Gethsemane. By doing so, he would have avoided the part of the seder immediately following, in which a door is opened for Elijah, whose visit to the celebration foreshadows his future arrival at the end of days, when he will come to announce the coming of the Messiah. There was

I. Kadeish (blessings and first cup of wine)
II. Ur'chatz (washing the hands)
III. Karpas (appetizer)
IV. Yachatz (breaking the middle matzah)
V. Magid (the telling)
1. Ha Lachma Anya (invitation to seder)
2. Ma Nistanah (The Four Questions)
3. The Four Sons
4. "Go and learn"
5. Kos Sheini (second cup of wine)
VI. Rohtzah (ritual washing of hands)
VII. Motzi ("who brings forth")
VIII. Matzo (blessing of the matzah)
IX. Maror (bitter herbs)
X. Koreich (the Hillel sandwich)
XI. Shulchan Orech (the meal)
XII. Tzafun (eating the afikomen)
XIII. Boreich (grace after meals)
1. Kos Shlishi (the third cup of wine)
2. Kos shel Eliyahu ha-Navi (Cup of Elijah)
XIV. Hallel (songs of praise)
XV. Nirtzah (concluding song and prayer)

✡ 31 ✝

I. Kadeish (blessings and first cup of wine)
II. Ur'chatz (washing the hands)
III. Karpas (appetizer)
IV. Yachatz (breaking the middle matzah)
V. Magid (the telling)
1. Ha Lachma Anya (invitation to seder)
2. Ma Nistanah (The Four Questions)
3. The Four Sons
4. "Go and learn"
5. Kos Sheini (second cup of wine)
VI. Rohtzah (ritual washing of hands)
VII. Motzi ("who brings forth")
VIII. Matzo (blessing of the matzah)
IX. Maror (bitter herbs)
X. Koreich (the Hillel sandwich)
XI. Shulchan Orech (the meal)
XII. Tzafun (eating the afikomen)
XIII. Boreich (grace after meals)
1. Kos Shlishi (the third cup of wine)
2. Kos shel Eliyahu ha-Navi (Cup of Elijah)
XIV. Hallel (songs of praise)
XV. Nirtzah (concluding song and prayer)

no reason to open the door for Elijah at the Last Supper, since the Messiah was then present.[14]

It is interesting that Judas drank the second cup (the cup of judgment) but left the table before the third cup (the cup of redemption), whereas Jesus drank the third cup but refused more wine, even on the Cross [Matthew 27:34], until he would drink it "new with you in my Father's kingdom" [Matthew 26:29; cf. Mark 14:25]. At Gethsemane, Jesus prayed, "My Father, if it be possible, let this cup pass from me; nevertheless, not as I will, but as thou wilt" [Matthew 26:39; see also Mark 14:36 and Luke 22:42].

XIII. Bareich (grace after meals)
2. Kos shel Eliyahu ha-Navi (Cup of Elijah)

THEN ONE OF THE CHILDREN OPENS THE FRONT DOOR TO ALLOW ELIJAH TO COME TO THE SEDER AND DRINK FROM THE CUP OF ELIJAH PLACED ON THE TABLE.

Pour out thy anger on the nations
that do not know thee,
and on the kingdoms
that do not call on thy name!
For they have devoured Jacob,
and laid waste his habitation. [Psalm 79:6–7]

---

[14] When Jesus was on the Cross, he quoted the first line of the 22nd Psalm, "Eli Eli lama sabachthani" (this from Matthew's Gospel; it is slightly different in Mark's), which some of the witnesses thought was a cry to Elijah. Psalm 22 recreates beautifully the Haggadah's two halves: first, sorrow and slavery; then, redemption and salvation (because it is so important, the full psalm is enclosed:

My God, my God, why hast thou forsaken me?
Why art thou so far from helping me, from the words of my groaning?
O my God, I cry by day, but thou dost not answer;
and by night, but find no rest.
Yet thou art holy,

Pour out thy indignation upon them,
and let thy burning anger overtake them. [Psalm
69:24]

---

enthroned on the praises of Israel.
In thee our fathers trusted;
they trusted, and thou didst deliver them.
To thee they cried, and were saved;
in thee they trusted, and were not disappointed.
But I am a worm, and no man;
scorned by men, and despised by the people.
All who see me mock at me,
they make mouths at me, they wag their heads;
"He committed his cause to the LORD; let him deliver him,
let him rescue him, for he delights in him!"
Yet thou art he who took me from the womb;
thou didst keep me safe upon my mother's breasts.
Upon thee was I cast from my birth,
and since my mother bore me thou hast been my God.
Be not far from me,
for trouble is near
and there is none to help.
Many bulls encompass me,
strong bulls of Bashan surround me;
they open wide their mouths at me,
like a ravening and roaring lion.
I am poured out like water,
and all my bones are out of joint;
my heart is like wax,
it is melted within my breast;
my strength is dried up like a potsherd,
and my tongue cleaves to my jaws;
thou dost lay me in the dust of death.
Yea, dogs are round about me;
a company of evildoers encircle me;
they have pierced my hands and feet –
I can count all my bones –
they stare and gloat over me;
they divide my garments among them,
and for my raiment they cast lots.
But thou, O LORD, be not far off!
O thou my help, hasten to my aid!
Deliver my soul from the sword,
my life from the power of the dog!
Save me from the mouth of the lion,
my afflicted soul from the horns of the wild oxen!
I will tell of thy name to my brethren;
in the midst of the congregation I will praise thee:
You who fear the LORD, praise him!
all you sons of Jacob, glorify him,

✡ 33 †

Thou wilt pursue them in anger and destroy them from under thy heavens, O LORD. [Lamentations 3:66]

CLOSE THE DOOR.

XIV. Hallel (songs of praise)

FILL THE FOURTH CUP AND SAY:

It is traditional that all of Psalms 115–118 are recited.
Not to us, O LORD, not to us,
but to thy name give glory,
for the sake of thy steadfast love and thy faithfulness!
Why should the nations say,
"Where is their God?"
Our God is in the heavens;
he does whatever he pleases.

———————

and stand in awe of him, all you sons of Israel!
For he has not despised or abhorred
the affliction of the afflicted;
and he has not hid his face from him,
but has heard, when he cried to him.
From thee comes my praise in the great congregation;
my vows I will pay before those who fear him.
The afflicted shall eat and be satisfied;
those who seek him shall praise the LORD!
May your hearts live for ever!
All the ends of the earth shall remember
and turn to the LORD;
and all the families of the nations
shall worship before him.
For dominion belongs to the LORD,
and he rules over the nations.
Yea, to him shall all the proud of the earth bow down;
before him shall bow all who go down to the dust,
and he who cannot keep himself alive.
Posterity shall serve him;
men shall tell of the Lord to the coming generation,
and proclaim his deliverance to a people yet unborn,
that he has wrought it. [Psalm 22]

Their idols are silver and gold,
the work of men's hands.
They have mouths, but do not speak;
eyes, but do not see.
They have ears, but do not hear;
noses, but do not smell.
They have hands, but do not feel;
feet, but do not walk;
and they do not make a sound in their throat.
Those who make them are like them;
so are all who trust in them.
O Israel, trust in the LORD!
He is their help and their shield.
O house of Aaron, put your trust in the LORD!
He is their help and their shield.
You who fear the LORD, trust in the LORD!
He is their help and their shield.
The LORD has been mindful of us; he will bless us;
he will bless the house of Israel;
he will bless the house of Aaron;
he will bless those who fear the LORD,
both small and great.
May the LORD give you increase,
you and your children!
May you be blessed by the LORD,
who made heaven and earth!
The heavens are the LORD's heavens,
but the earth he has given to the sons of men.
The dead do not praise the LORD,
nor do any that go down into silence.
But we will bless the LORD
from this time forth and for evermore.
Praise the LORD! [Psalm 115]

The Lord has remembered us. He will bless us, he
will bless the house of Israel, he will bless the house

of Aaron. He will bless those who revere the Lord, the small as well as the great: May the Lord increase you, more and more, you and your children. You are blessed of the Lord, the maker of heaven and earth. The heavens are the heavens of the Lord, but the earth he has given to the children of men. The dead praise not the Lord, nor do they who descend into the silent grave. But we will bless the Lord, from henceforth until evermore. Hallelujah.

I love the LORD, because he has heard
my voice and my supplications.
Because he inclined his ear to me,
therefore I will call on him as long as I live.
The snares of death encompassed me;
the pangs of Sheol laid hold on me;
I suffered distress and anguish.
Then I called on the name of the LORD:
"O LORD, I beseech thee, save my life!"
Gracious is the LORD, and righteous;
our God is merciful.
The LORD preserves the simple;
when I was brought low, he saved me.
Return, O my soul, to your rest;
for the LORD has dealt bountifully with you.
For thou hast delivered my soul from death,
my eyes from tears,
my feet from stumbling;
I walk before the LORD
in the land of the living.
I kept my faith, even when I said,
"I am greatly afflicted";
I said in my consternation,
"Men are all a vain hope."
What shall I render to the LORD
for all his bounty to me?

I will lift up the cup of salvation
and call on the name of the LORD,
I will pay my vows to the LORD
in the presence of all his people.
Precious in the sight of the LORD
is the death of his saints.
O LORD, I am thy servant;
I am thy servant, the son of thy handmaid.
Thou hast loosed my bonds.
I will offer to thee the sacrifice of thanksgiving
and call on the name of the LORD.
I will pay my vows to the LORD
in the presence of all his people,
in the courts of the house of the LORD,
in your midst, O Jerusalem.
Praise the LORD! [Psalm 116]

Praise the LORD, all nations!
Extol him, all peoples!
For great is his steadfast love toward us;
and the faithfulness of the LORD endures for ever.
Praise the LORD! [Psalm 117]

O give thanks to the LORD, for he is good;
his steadfast love endures for ever!
Let Israel say,
"His steadfast love endures for ever."
Let the house of Aaron say,
"His steadfast love endures for ever."
Let those who fear the LORD say,
"His steadfast love endures for ever."
Out of my distress I called on the LORD;
the LORD answered me and set me free.
With the LORD on my side I do not fear.
What can man do to me?
The LORD is on my side to help me;

I shall look in triumph on those who hate me.
It is better to take refuge in the LORD
than to put confidence in man.
It is better to take refuge in the LORD
than to put confidence in princes.
All nations surrounded me;
in the name of the LORD I cut them off!
They surrounded me, surrounded me on every side;
in the name of the LORD I cut them off!
They surrounded me like bees,
they blazed like a fire of thorns;
in the name of the LORD I cut them off!
I was pushed hard, so that I was falling,
but the LORD helped me.
The LORD is my strength and my song;
he has become my salvation.
Hark, glad songs of victory
in the tents of the righteous:
"The right hand of the LORD does valiantly,
the right hand of the LORD is exalted,
the right hand of the LORD does valiantly!"
I shall not die, but I shall live,
and recount the deeds of the LORD.
The LORD has chastened me sorely,
but he has not given me over to death.
Open to me the gates of righteousness,
that I may enter through them
and give thanks to the LORD.
This is the gate of the LORD;
the righteous shall enter through it.
I thank thee that thou hast answered me
and hast become my salvation.
The stone which the builders rejected
has become the head of the corner.
This is the LORD's doing;
it is marvelous in our eyes.

This is the day which the LORD has made;
let us rejoice and be glad in it.
Save us, we beseech thee, O LORD!
O LORD, we beseech thee, give us success!
Blessed be he who enters in the name of the
LORD!
We bless you from the house of the LORD.
The LORD is God,
and he has given us light.
Bind the festal procession with branches,
up to the horns of the altar!
Thou art my God, and I will give thanks to thee;
thou art my God, I will extol thee.
O give thanks to the LORD, for he is good;
for his steadfast love endures for ever! [Psalm 118]

All your works, O Lord, shall praise you; your pious servants with the righteous who perform your will, and your people, the house of Israel, with joyful song shall give thanks, bless, praise, glorify, extol, reverence, sanctify, and acknowledge your name. O our King, for to you it is good to render thanksgiving, and pleasant to sing praise to your name, for you are God from everlasting to everlasting.

There follows several other prayers, starting with Psalm 136, which is not unlike Psalm 118, plus several other prayers of praise.

O give thanks to the LORD, for he is good,
for his steadfast love endures for ever.
O give thanks to the God of gods,
for his steadfast love endures for ever.
O give thanks to the Lord of lords,
for his steadfast love endures for ever;
to him who alone does great wonders,
for his steadfast love endures for ever;
to him who by understanding made the heavens,
for his steadfast love endures for ever;
to him who spread out the earth upon the waters,

for his steadfast love endures for ever;

to him who made the great lights,

for his steadfast love endures for ever;

the sun to rule over the day,

for his steadfast love endures for ever;

the moon and stars to rule over the night,

for his steadfast love endures for ever;

to him who smote the first-born of Egypt,

for his steadfast love endures for ever;

and brought Israel out from among them,

for his steadfast love endures for ever;

with a strong hand and an outstretched arm,

for his steadfast love endures for ever;

to him who divided the Red Sea in sunder,

for his steadfast love endures for ever;

and made Israel pass through the midst of it,

for his steadfast love endures for ever;

but overthrew Pharaoh and his host in the Red Sea,

for his steadfast love endures for ever;

to him who led his people through the wilderness,

for his steadfast love endures for ever;

to him who smote great kings,

for his steadfast love endures for ever;

and slew famous kings,

for his steadfast love endures for ever;

Sihon, king of the Amorites,

for his steadfast love endures for ever;

and Og, king of Bashan,

for his steadfast love endures for ever;

and gave their land as a heritage,

for his steadfast love endures for ever;

a heritage to Israel his servant,

for his steadfast love endures for ever.

It is he who remembered us in our low estate,

for his steadfast love endures for ever;

and rescued us from our foes,

for his steadfast love endures for ever;

he who gives food to all flesh,

for his steadfast love endures for ever.

O give thanks to the God of heaven,

for his steadfast love endures for ever. (Psalm 136)

The soul of every living being shall bless your name, O Lord our God. The spirit of all flesh shall continually glorify and extol your name, our King. From eternity to eternity you are God, and beside you we have no king, redeemer, or savior. You are our Redeemer, Sustainer, Deliverer, and Merciful One in every time of trouble and distress. We have no king but you. You are God of the first and of the last; the God of all creatures, the Lord of all generations. You are adored with all manner of praise, who governs the universe with kindness and your creatures with mercy. The Lord neither slumbers nor sleeps; he rouses those who sleep and awakens those who slumber. He causes the dumb to speak and releases those who are bound. He supports the fallen and raises up those who are bowed down. To you alone we worship. Were our mouths filled with melodious songs, as the fullness of the sea; our tongues with shouting, as the raging waves; our lips with praise, as the wide-extended heavens; our eyes as brilliant as the sun and moon; our hands raised as the eagles fly heavenward; our feet as swift as a roe, we could not render sufficient thanks to you, O Lord our God and God of our fathers, and to praise your name for one of the countless deeds of love that you have conferred on us and our ancestors. For you, O Lord, our God, redeemed us from Egypt and released us from the house of bondage. In time of famine you sustained us, and in plenty nourished us. From the sword you delivered us, from pestilence you saved us, and from disease and raging sickness you relieved us. Until now your tender mercies have supported us, and your kindness has not forsaken us. O Lord our God do not forsake us in the future. Therefore , the limbs with which you formed us, the spirit and soul that you breathed into us, the tongue you placed in our mouth, they shall worship, bless, praise, glorify, extol, reverence, sanctify, and acknowledge your sovereign power, our King. Every mouth shall adore you; every tongue shall vow allegiance to you; every knee shall bend to you; all who stand erect shall bow down before you; every heart shall revere you; and all our inmost feelings and thoughts shall sing praises to your name, as it is written "All my bones shall say, 'O LORD, who is like thee, thou who deliverest the weak from him who is too strong for him, the weak and needy from him who despoils him?" [Psalm 35:10] Who is like you? who is equal to you? who can be compared to you? O great, mighty, and love-inspiring God! Maker of heaven and earth. We shall praise, adore, glorify, and bless your name, as it is said by David, "Bless the LORD, O my soul; and all that is within me, bless his holy name! [Psalm 103:1] For you O Lord are mighty in strength, great in your glorious name, powerful forever, and awful in your fearful deeds, O King who sits on the high and exalted throne.

He who abides forever, most exalted in his name, as it is written, "Rejoice in the LORD, O you righteous! Praise befits the upright." [Psalm 33:1] By the mouth of the upright shall you be praised, blessed by the utterances of the righteous, extolled by the tongue of the pious, and sanctified in the midst of saints.

And in the assemblies of the myriad of your people, the house of Israel, your name will be glorified, O our King, throughout all generations, for it is the duty of all created beings in your present, O Lord our God and the God of our fathers, to extol, honor, bless, exalt, magnify, glorify with song beyond all the utterances of the hymns and psalms of David the son of Jesse, your servant and your anointed.

Praised be your name forever, O our King! God and King, great and holy, in heaven and on earth! for to you, O Lord our God and the God of our fathers, rightly belongs song and praise, hymn and psalm; strength and dominion; victory, greatness and power, adoration and glory; sanctity and majesty; laud and thanksgiving henceforth and forever more. Blessed are you, O Lord, Almighty King glorified with praises, worthy of great thanksgiving, Lord of wondrous deeds, who delights in songs of psalmody; King, Almighty, and Eternal.

There are a number of prayers that follow that may be considered of lesser import, so we have put them at the end of the service.

Blessed are you, O Lord our God, King of the Universe, creator of the fruit of the vine.

בָּרוּךְ אַתָּה יְיָ אֱלֹהֵינוּ מֶלֶךְ הָעוֹלָם בּוֹרֵא פְּרִי הַגָּפֶן:

BAW-RUCH A-TAW A-DO-NOI EL-O-HA-NU ME-LECH HAW-O-LAWM BO-RAY P'-REE HA-GAW-FEN.

DRINK THE FOURTH CUP OF WINE AND SAY:

The underlined passage is said on the Sabbath only.
Blessed are you, O Lord our God, King of the Universe, for the wine and for the fruit of the vine and for the produce of the field and for that desirable, good, and spacious land which you granted our ancestors to inherit, to eat of its fruit and be satisfied with its goodness. Have compassion, O Lord our God, on us, on Israel your people, on Jerusalem your city, on Zion the residence of your glory, and on your altar and temple. Rebuild Jerusalem, your holy city, speedily, in our days. (<u>Be gracious to us and give us strength and</u>) cheer us on this day of the feast of the unleavened bread, for you, O Lord our God, are good and beneficent to all, and therefore we give thanks to you for the land and for the fruit of the vine. Blessed are you, O Lord our God, for the land and the fruit of the vine.

XV. Nirtzah *(concluding song and prayer)*

The commemoration service of the Passover has now been accomplished according to its order, all the ordinances and customs of the feast. As we have been deemed worthy to prepare it now, grant also that we may be worthy to fulfill it. You, O Most Holy who dwells on high, raise up your people, the innumerable. O hasten to conduct us, the plants of your vineyard, once more redeemed to Zion with joyful song.

O may he who is most mighty soon rebuild his house; speedily, speedily, soon, in our days; O God, rebuild it, O Lord, rebuild it, rebuild your house in good time.

O may he who is supreme, the greatest and most exalted, soon rebuild his house, speedily, speedily, soon, in our days. O God, rebuild it, O Lord, rebuild it, rebuild your house in good time.

May he who is all-honored and worthy, most immaculate and merciful, soon rebuild his house, speedily, speedily, soon, in our days. O God, rebuild it, O Lord, rebuild it, rebuild your house in good time.

May he who is most pure, the sole God, soon rebuild his house, speedily, speedily, soon, in our days. O God, rebuild it, O Lord, rebuild it, rebuild your house in good time.

May he who is all-powerful, omnipotent, and all-ruling, soon rebuild his house, speedily, speedily, soon, in our days. O God, rebuild it, O Lord, rebuild it, rebuild your house in good time.

May he who is most glorious and elevated, the eternal of strength, soon rebuild his house, speedily, speedily, soon, in our days. O God, rebuild it, O Lord, rebuild it, rebuild your house in good time.

May he who is the Redeemer, the all-righteous, the Most Holy, soon rebuild his house, speedily, speedily, soon, in our days. O God, rebuild it, O Lord, rebuild it, rebuild your house in good time.

May he who is the most compassionate, the Almighty, Omnipotent, soon rebuild his house, speedily, speedily, soon, in our days. O God, rebuild it, O Lord, rebuild it, rebuild your house in good time.

The following prayer may be said the first night of Passover.
And thus it came to pass at midnight. Of old you performed abundant miracles in the night, at the beginning of the first watch of this night. When you caused Abraham, the true convert, to be victorious when he divided his company at night. It was at midnight.

You threatened the king of Gerar (Abimelech) with death in a dream at night. You terrified the Syrian (Laban) in the night. And Israel (Jacob) wrestled with the angel and prevailed against him at night. It was at midnight.

The first born of the Egyptians you smote at midnight. Their vigorous youth they did not find when they arose at midnight. The army of the prince of Harosheth you trampled down through the stars at night. It was at midnight.

When the blaspheming Senachereb sought to assail your habitation, you frustrated him by the number of the dead, in the night. Ba'al and its image were overthrown in the darkness of night. To the much-beloved man (Daniel) was the mysterious vision revealed at night. It was at midnight.

He who made himself drunken out of the holy vessels was slain in that same night. He (Daniel) was delivered from the lion's den, he who interpreted the terrifying dreams of the night. Haman the Agagite, who cherished enmity, wrote his letters to exterminate the Jews, at night. It was at midnight.

You awakened your all-conquering power against him by disturbing the sleep of the king at night. You will tread the winepress for them, who ask, "watchmen, what of the night?" Let the Lord, the Watchman of Israel, cry out, the morning has come as well as the night. It was at midnight.

O may the day of redemption approach, which shall be neither day nor night. Make known, O Most High, that yours is the day and the night. Appoint watchmen to your city (Jerusalem) all day and all night. Illuminate, as with the light of day, the darkness of our night. It was at midnight.

For the second night.
You shall say this is the sacrifice of the Passover.
Your mighty power you displayed on the Passover.
To be the chief of all the solemn feasts you exalted the Passover.
You revealed to the Oriental (Abraham) the miracles performed at midnight at the Passover.
And you shall say this is the sacrifice of the Passover.

You visited his (Abraham's) door during the heat of the day at the Passover.

He entertained the angels with unleavened cakes at the Passover.

To the herd he ran and prepared a calf, a prototype of the sacrifice of the Passover.

The Sodomites provoked God, and were consumed with fire at the Passover.

Lot was delivered from them, and he baked unleavened cakes at the Passover.

You swept the land of Moph and Noph when you passed through it at the Passover.

And you shall say this is the sacrifice of the Passover.

Lord, you smote the head of every first-born on the night of the Passover.

You passed, O Omnipotent, over the first-born (Israel) marked with the blood of the sacrifice of the Passover.

Not suffering the destroyer to enter within my doors, at the Passover.

And you shall say this is the sacrifice of the Passover.

The strongly besieged city (Jericho) was surrendered at the Passover.

Midian was destroyed by the cake of barley bread, like the offering of an Omer, at the Passover.

The mighty of Pul and Lud were destroyed with burning conflagration, on the Passover.

And you shall say this is the sacrifice of the Passover.

He (the King) remained yet in Nob till the approach of the Passover.

The hand wrote the extermination of Babylon, the deep abyss at the Passover.

The "watch was then set" and "the table then spread" at the Passover.

And you shall say this is the sacrifice of the Passover.

Hadassah (Esther) assembled the congregation to fast three days at the Passover.

The sworn enemy (Haman) you caused to be executed on the gallows fifty cubits high, at the Passover.

The double punishment will you in a moment bring on Urz at the Passover.

Your hand will then show itself omnipotent, and your right hand be exalted as on the night when was the celebration of the Festival of the Passover.

And you shall say this is the sacrifice of the Passover.

On both nights, say:

To him praise is becoming. To him praise will always be becoming.

He is all powerful in his kingdom; he is essentially supreme, his angelic hosts say to him: Yours and yours only; yours, yes, yours; yours, surely yours; yours, O Lord, is the sovereignty. To him praise is becoming. To him praise will always be becoming.

His is most high in his kingdom; he is most glorious; his servants say to him: Yours and yours only; yours, yes, yours; yours, surely yours; yours, O Lord, is the sovereignty. To him praise is becoming. To him praise will always be becoming.

He is pure in his kingdom; he is Most Mighty, his angels say to him: Yours and yours only; yours, yes, yours; yours, surely yours; yours, O Lord, is the sovereignty. To him praise is becoming. To him praise will always be becoming.

He is the one in his Kingdom; he is Omnipotent; they say to him: Yours and yours only; yours, yes, yours; yours, surely yours; yours, O Lord, is the sovereignty. To him praise is becoming. To him praise will always be becoming.

He is the Ruler in his kingdom; he is the most awful; the hosts surrounding him say: Yours and yours only; yours, yes, yours; yours, surely yours; yours, O Lord, is the sovereignty. To him praise is becoming. To him praise will always be becoming.

He is the most meek in his kingdom; he is the Redeemer; the righteous say: Yours and yours only; yours, yes, yours; yours, surely yours; yours, O Lord, is the sovereignty. To him praise is becoming. To him praise will always be becoming.

He is the most Holy in his kingdom; he is the most merciful; the "Shinanim" say: Yours and yours only; yours, yes, yours; yours, surely yours; yours, O Lord, is the sovereignty. To Him praise is becoming. To Him praise will always be becoming.

He is the Almighty in his kingdom; he is the upholder of the perfect, who say to him: Yours and yours only; yours, yes, yours; yours, surely yours; yours, O Lord, is the sovereignty. To him praise is becoming. To him praise will always be becoming.

The house of my soul is too small to receive Thee; let it be enlarged by Thee. It is all in ruins; do Thou repair it. (Confessions of St. Augustine I, v)

Gratitude should not take a back seat to anything in our lives, much less a back page, but here it sits, no less for faith, hope, and charity than if it was placed on the cover.

Fr. Daniel Scheidt was most helpful in both his encouragement and his corrections. We are all in need of great models in life; he is one.

Scott Brown, National Director of Celebrate Messiah, New Zealand (an organization in partnership with similar ministries in thirteen countries, all of them under the umbrella of Chosen People Global Ministries), did more than critique and suggest – he ended up writing several important sections in the book that greatly enhanced its message. His is the kind of knowledge that opens the heart as much as the mind.